D1826988

This book belongs to

Name

Address

Telephone No.

My plans for Christmas

Also in this series:
My Friend's Address Book   My Travel Book   My Autograph Book
Published simultaneously in 1994 by Exley Publications in Great Britain,
and Exley Giftbooks in the USA.
Edited by Helen Exley.   **Illustrated by Angela Kerr.**
Copyright © Helen Exley 1994.
The moral right of the author has been asserted.
ISBN 1-85015-955-6
A copy of the CIP data is available from the British Library on request. All rights reserved.
No part of this publication may be reproduced or transmitted in any form or by any means,
electronic or mechanical, including photocopy, recording or any information storage and retrieval
system without permission in writing from the publisher.

Typeset by Delta, Watford.
Printed and bound in Malta.

2   4   6   8   10   12   11   9   7   5   3   1

Exley Publications Ltd, 16 Chalk Hill, Watford, Herts WD1 4BN
Exley Publications LLC, 232 Madison Avenue, Suite 1206, NY 10016, USA.

MY CHRISTMAS BOOK

A record book with plans for a happy,
creative Christmas

Edited by Helen Exley, illustrated by Angela Kerr

EXLEY

NEW YORK • WATFORD, UK

CONTENTS

Introduction

There's so much to remember at Christmas time and planning sometimes needs to be done weeks in advance. This little book will help you make sure you don't forget anything – there's a special place for you to write lists of people you need to send cards to and a column for you to fill in with ideas for gifts. As well as helping you get organized, there are exciting ideas for making your own decorations, wrapping paper and even a festive Christmas tree frieze! Then there's a list for you to fill in to make sure that you don't miss anyone out with your "thank-yous"! And when it's all over there's a space for you to stick a special picture. The finished book makes a lovely souvenir of your Christmas that you can share with faraway friends and relatives.

Fill in this book carefully and you'll see that planning and preparing for Christmas can be just as much fun as the big day itself. Merry Christmas!

Helen Exley

Christmas card list

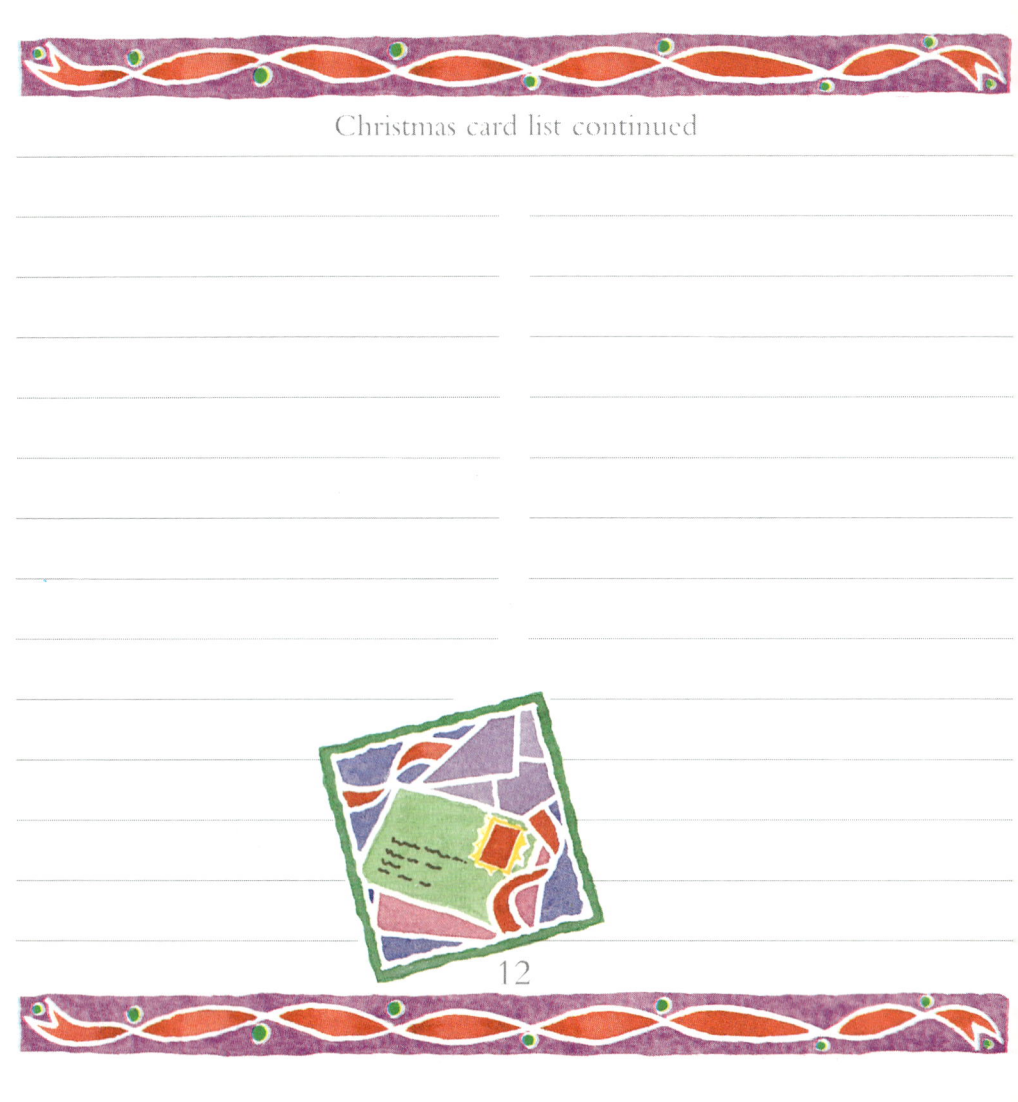

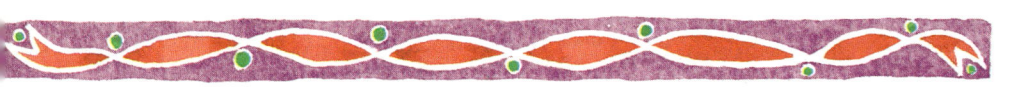

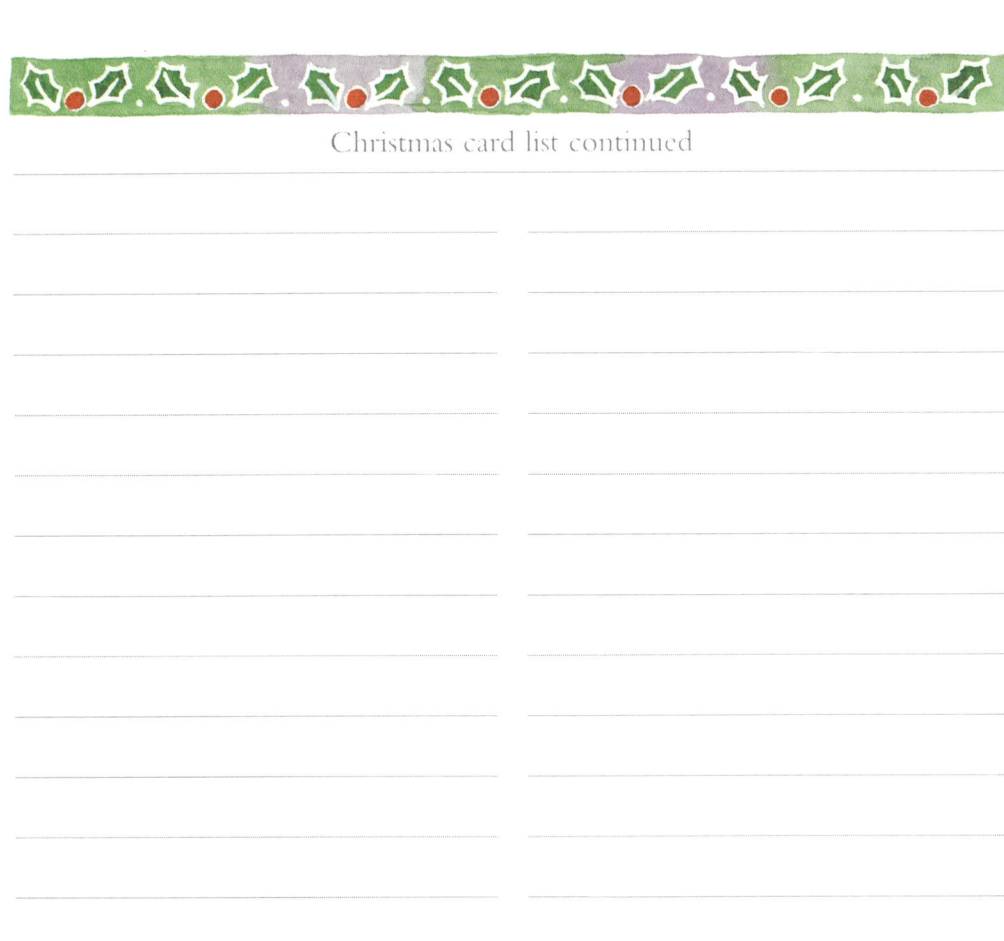

Christmas card list continued

Here is a super Christmas card to make

1. Fold a piece of cardboard or stiff paper in half, and decorate it with a bright pattern.

2. On another piece of card draw a Santa Claus – you can copy ours.

3. Ask a grown-up to help you cut him out.

4. Glue your Santa Claus onto the front of your card. You could decorate his hat with a cotton ball – or sprinkle him with glitter to finish off.

Christmas gift list

Name	Idea	Bought/Made	Wrapped

Making your own wrapping paper

1. Cut a potato in half.

2. Choose a Christmas shape. We chose a tree – you could have a star, a bell or a holly leaf. Draw this onto the cut half of your potato or instead of drawing you could use a Christmas pastry cutter to make your shape. Ask a grown-up to cut away the potato from the edge of your shape, so that it is raised up – make sure there is enough left at the back of the potato for you to hold!

3. Dip your potato shape into poster paint.

4. Press the painted shape firmly onto a piece of plain paper to get a good print. Do this all over the paper to make a pattern.

5. To make your wrapping paper more exciting you could add extra decorations with bright felt pens and crayons.

★ **Make sure there is a grown-up to help you cut the potato.**

17

Christmas gift list continued

Name	Idea	Bought/Made	Wrapped

Christmas gifts I liked most and why

Gift tags to make

Use your potato print to make gift
tags to match your wrapping paper.
Cut some pieces of cardboard into
squares or Christmas shapes, and
using bright paint decorate them with your potato
print. Punch a hole in the corner and thread with
some ribbon or string.

19

Decorations needed!

_____

_____

_____

_____

_____

_____

_____

How to make a Christmas tree frieze

1. Fold a long piece of green paper into an accordion.

2. Draw a Christmas tree on the first page and carefully cut round it. Make sure you don't cut completely through the edges at either side of the tree.

3. When you unfold the paper there should be a row of trees all joined together. You could decorate your frieze with glitter or bright sticky paper shapes.

20

Christmas tree decorations

Christmas tree decorations continued

Ideas from the kitchen

If a grown-up is making some cookie dough, ask if you can have some to make these special Christmas biscuits.

Roll the dough out and make it into stars, bells, hearts or any Christmassy shapes. Make a little hole in each cookie before they are baked so that you can thread them with ribbon and hang them on the Christmas tree when they are finished.

When the cookies have been baked and are cool, you can start to decorate them. Coat them in bright icing or frosting, and stick on silver balls or sugar strands.

You can decorate small sponge cakes or shortbread in the same way as the cookies. Use white icing or frosting to look like snow, make holly leaf shapes out of green marzipan and add small pieces of cherry to look like berries.

These pretty cakes and cookies make super gifts for friends and relatives.

The Christmas Day table decorations

A photo or drawing of this special Christmas

Remember for next Christmas

Thank-you list

Notes